The Chokehold

Earl Ofari Hutchinson

Publisher's Cataloging-in-Publication Data

Names: Hutchinson, Earl Ofari.
Title: The Chokehold / Earl Ofari Hutchinson.
Description: Los Angeles, CA : Middle Passage Press,
    2023. | Includes bibliographic references and index.
Identifiers: LCCN 2023909355| ISBN 979-8-89074-
    611-5 (pbk.)
Subjects: LCSH: -- Political aspects. | Politics-|
    Discrimination| | BISAC: Political Science / Civil
    Rights / POLITICAL SCIENCE / civil rights/
    General. | POLITICS / Social Aspects.
Classification: LCC GV1318.H88 2023 | DDC 794.1 H--
dc23
LC record available at https://lccn.loc.gov/2023909355

Table of Contents

About the Author

"The victim's face turns blue as he is deprived of oxygen. He goes into spasmodic convulsions. His eyes rolled back. His body wriggles. His feet kick up and down. His arms move about wildly."

LAPD Officer Amusingly Describing the Chokehold

Introduction

In May 1982, the feisty, controversial, and frequently embattled Los Angeles Police Chief Daryl F. Gates found himself again on the public and national media hot seat. In an interview with the *Los Angeles Times*, Gates said, "We may be finding that in some blacks when it (the chokehold) is applied, the veins and arteries do not open as fast as they do in normal people."

Gates was ridiculed, hectored, and harangued by civil rights leaders, and many in the media, for his blatantly insensitive racist quip. He didn't back down from his pseudo anatomical, fallacious medical, just plain stupid, and colossal racist effort to justify a controversial and deadly police practice. That was the use of the chokehold.

Gates had repeatedly come under fire in prior years for authorizing and even applauding the use of multiple deadly type chokeholds on suspects. There were a lot of them. In the five years between 1975 and 1980, LAPD officers used chokeholds on nearly one thousand occasions. At least fifteen persons died because of the hold. Nearly all were Black men. The unapologetic Gates defended the use of the hold as the more benign way to subdue a suspect. To him, it was a tactic that did less physical harm to someone than presumably the gun or the club.

Gates was hardly a lone voice within police ranks cheerleading the use of the deadly chokehold. Numerous police departments at the time of the Gates inflammatory flap on the chokehold, and in the decades after, also authorized and even encouraged their officers to use the hold. Predictably, the widespread use of the chokehold by police resulted in many severe injuries and deaths.

Some departments during those years backed off and either restricted the use of the hold or barred it. It took the national furor over the choking death of George Floyd by then Minneapolis police officer Derek Chauvin in May 2020 for a torrent of police departments to scrap the use of the chokehold. By the middle of 2021, twenty-four states had restricted or banned outright the use of chokeholds and other neck restraints.

Yet, more than two dozen other states hadn't banned the hold. Even with the Floyd turmoil and a major push for police reform, there was no consensus, let alone prohibition, on whether the chokehold should be totally outlawed.

A SCOTUS ruling on the use of the chokehold in 1983 further muddled the issue. By a 5 to 4 decision the court did not prohibit the use of the chokehold. That's where things remained in 2023, three years after Floyd. It took the choking slaying on a New York City subway train of Jordan Neely in May 2023 by former Marine Daniel Penny to again ram the issue of the chokehold back into the national debate.

In *The Chokehold*, political analyst Earl Ofari Hutchinson details the controversy over police and civilian use of chokeholds, how the courts, the police, and the public view the use of chokeholds, and the always lurking issue of racial bias in its use. Hutchinson asks, is it a legitimate tactic to protect, or a deadly cause of physical mayhem? *The Chokehold* confronts that challenging and troubling question.

1

The Enduring Life of the Chokehold

In May 2023, nine years had passed since NYPD officer Daniel Pantaleo choked street seller Eric Garner to death. The same month and year, exactly three years had passed since Minneapolis police officer, Derek Chauvin choked George Floyd to death. The passage of time and the date were important for two reasons.

It was the month that ex-Marine Daniel Penny choked homeless, mentally challenged, Jordan Neely to death. The second was the use of the deadly chokehold. It ignited rage, anger, and a national debate once more on the use of the chokehold and the potentially deadly consequence of it. Fueling the debate and anger, the three victims of the chokehold were African American men. Critics again charged that the chokehold was a racially skewed lethal tactic targeting Black men.

Following the choking death of Garner in 2014, some police departments publicly declared that they did not use the chokehold. They waved and cited inter-department regulation after regulation to prove that they barred the use of the hold, didn't teach it to officers, and that many officers themselves said they wouldn't know how to use it anyway.

That part, namely teaching the proper use of the technique, was certainly true. However, the chokehold was still in widespread use in police departments. It had many vigorous defenders. They gave a litany of reasons why the chokehold was supposedly a vital weapon in law enforcement's arsenal.

*****

One police department, though not American, had a long and storied reputation as a model of police efficiency. That was the Royal Canadian Mounted Police. It too was concerned about the potentially deadly effect of the use of the chokehold. In June 2020, one month after Floyd's death, the RCMP commissioned a study on the use of the chokehold.

In the meantime, it decided not to bar the use of the hold. It presented the by-then-stock reasons police officials gave for its continued use. The first was to assure that the chokehold was used only when there was the threat of grave injury, or bodily harm to the officer or someone else from an assailant.

The second reason was that the department, mindful of Chauvin's placement of his knee on Floyd's neck, took great pains to insist that it did not teach or endorse any technique where officers put a knee on a suspect's neck or head.

Finally, it maintained that officers only used a neck restraint as a measure to "maintain peace, order, and security." However, the agency then fell back on the standard argument purportedly based on medical research that the neck restraint technique the department used was not a chokehold when applied properly.

This was a crucial point of departure, and the fine line, between an alleged non-lethal use of the restraint, to the deadly use of it. The RCMP insisted that its officers were expertly trained in the proper use of a neck restraint. And that they were required to be retrained and certified every three years in the use of restraints.

Officials said that the department's criminal operations directorate, and police intervention trainers did an exacting review whenever an officer used the chokehold. The aim was twofold. One was to determine whether the procedure was used properly and whether there was any injury sustained. The other aim was to determine if the hold was used only to prevent serious bodily harm or injury to the officer or others.

RCMP officials were careful to state that the department used the chokehold in only a tiny number of cases. The number they cited, though, was much too small to determine if a neck restraint whether used properly or not was a safe technique to de-escalate an encount

*****

It was a far different matter though with many U.S. police departments. The substantial number of lawsuits brought by victims of the chokehold against departments at various times over the years before and after Garners' slaying showed that some departments and officers did use the chokehold or a variant of it to subdue suspects.

The U.S. Supreme Court made that possible. Nearly four decades earlier in 1983, it could have ended the use of the chokehold. It didn't. It rejected a lawsuit by Adolph Lyons, a young African American motorist, who was subjected to a chokehold by an LAPD officer following a traffic stop. The court ruled in a five to four decision against sustaining an injunction sought to bar its use. SCOTUS

Justice Thurgood Marshall in his dissenting opinion was prescient in how the chokehold would cause much legal mischief in the decades to come.

"Since no one can show that he will be choked in the future, no one – not even a person who, like Lyons, has almost been choked to death – has standing to challenge the continuation of the policy. The city is free to continue the policy indefinitely, as long as it is willing to pay damages for the injuries and deaths that result."

The Lyons case is detailed later.

Erwin Chemerinsky, the dean of the School of Law at the University of California, Berkeley agreed. In his book, *Presumed Guilty: How the*

Supreme Court Empowered the Police and Subverted Civil Rights, proved Marshall more than correct. He noted, "To give one example: George Floyd died in Minneapolis from police use of the chokehold. Eric Garner died in New York City from police use of a chokehold. Many others, especially Black men, have died from police use of the chokehold. One would wonder: Why hasn't the Supreme Court said that the chokehold violates the Constitution, that there have been lawsuits trying to enjoin police use of the chokehold?"

This is the question that remains both puzzling, frustrating, and largely unanswered on the issue of police reform. It's a question, sadly, that the SCOTUS and other courts have answered with their rulings and decisions to permit the continued use of the chokehold. It's a question, equally sadly answered by many police departments in the U.S. that refuse to bar the use of the chokehold. In the meantime, the Floyds and Neely's continue to be the victims of its use

2

What Doctors Say About Chokeholds

Within weeks after the Floyd slaying the San Diego Police Department banned the use of the chokehold. Several prominent medical experts consulted reaffirmed that the chokehold was a lethal technique that could cause injury or death.

One of the experts, James Santiago Grisolia, *a prominent neurologist, reviewed the medical hazards that the use of the technique posed. But Santiago also warned that it was* impossible to know the true numerator or denominator of medical complications from carotid restraints, as most cases go unreported except in a very anecdotal fashion.

This made it even more imperative for medical experts to firmly establish the lethal nature of the chokehold precisely because of its still widespread use and lack of knowledge of its hazard. How many individuals were still victims of the chokehold? In the decades after Lyons in 1976 sought an injunction to bar the LAPD from using it, doctors and medical practitioners, criminologists, and scientists had frequently assessed the medical hazard of the technique.

*****

There was no surprise that there was sharp division and debate over not only whether chokeholds wreak the physical damage claimed, but whether they could be used even with proper training to minimize injury. There was more debate over the attempt to make distinctions between the types of chokeholds used.

Some experts argued that there are different types of neck restraints in which breathing, and blood flow are not cut off or impaired. They supposedly did not cause major neck and throat injuries. The term "neck restraint" encompassed two types of compressions: strangleholds, which block blood flow to the brain through two pressure points on the neck, and chokeholds, which bar airflow through the windpipe.

However, while there was much hair-splitting on whether with the right training and a benign grip, no injury or harm would result, there was no debate that a carotid chokehold that cuts off breath by applying force to the throat or windpipe could maim or kill.

The Justice Department and the American Academy of Neurology in 2021 conducted a rigorous study of the medical hazards of the carotid restraint. They were emphatic. The choke grip is "inherently dangerous." They added that the hold that results in loss of oxygen or blood flow could cause permanent injury to the brain, including stroke, cognitive disability, or death. A lack of training using the grip could increase the likelihood of death.

The Academy flatly called on law enforcement to classify "neck restraints, at a minimum, as a form of deadly force." It added, "There is no amount of training or method of application of neck restraints that can mitigate the risk of death or permanent profound neurologic damage with this maneuver."

In other words, the tactic should be banned totally. The Academy, significantly, did not try to find any gray area in the use of the chokehold. It did not soften the danger of the hold. For the Academy, no amount of expert training or applying a benign grip could avoid the risk of injury.

A team of Boston neurologists came to the same conclusion. In December 2020, they published their findings in the *Journal of the American Medical Association.* Jillian Berkman, one of the neurologists involved in the study was specific, "The whole importance of the blood flow itself is that the blood is what's carrying the oxygen, so if you're not getting blood up to the brain, you're not getting oxygen to the brain." Berkman added, "The end result could still be the same as when you're choking someone. Both chokeholds and strangleholds have the potential to be deadly."

The researchers pointed out that the brain requires fifteen to twenty percent of the blood in circulation to properly function, and this blood predominately travels through the two carotid arteries—both of which are blocked during strangleholds. This interruption can cause multiple medical malfunctions, including seizures, strokes, arrhythmias, and vascular damage.

*****

Much of the prior medical research on the use of chokeholds almost exclusively focused on the damage physical potential of a chokehold. However, there was also the devastating psychological trauma a chokehold could cause.

Jaime Zuckerman, a clinical psychologist, and an expert on trauma was deeply disturbed by the adverse psychological effect a chokehold could have on an individual. She noted that psychological traumas often result from an individual being physically incapacitated even momentarily. This radically increased their vulnerability.

"Any type of sudden or threatened physical attack or violation can lead to trauma responses. Post-traumatic stress disorder (PTSD), acute stress disorder, panic disorder, and even depression can develop in response to such an event." Zuckerman emphasized, "The resulting mental health symptoms can have far-reaching implications, particularly within populations where mental health treatment is difficult to access and/or there is a significant stigma surrounding mental health. This not only makes it less likely that people will seek treatment but also increases the risk of substance abuse as a way to self-medicate."

The most important finding in the studies of the effect of a chokehold was that a person could die from it in a matter of moments. In fact, it could be seconds, four seconds to be exact. That was the case with Garner. It took barely one minute for the hold to trigger his death. In the case of Floyd, the eight minutes and forty-six seconds he was choked was an incredible one hundred times longer than what is necessary to make a victim lose consciousness.

*****

The detailed studies conducted by medical personnel on the damage caused by chokeholds were conclusive enough for

President Biden. On the second anniversary of the chokehold slaying of Floyd, in May 2022, he signed an executive order banning the chokehold by federal law enforcement. The only exception it could be used was when an officer's life was in mortal danger.

Biden made clear the chokehold was one of the major causes of the chronic rancor between police and minority communities, "Police cannot fulfill their role to keep communities safe without public trust and confidence in law enforcement and the criminal justice system. Yet, there are places in America today where the bonds of trust are frayed or broken. To heal as a nation, we must acknowledge that fatal encounters with law enforcement have disproportionately involved Black and Brown people."

The Justice Department went a step further. In 2021 it concluded that both chokeholds and carotid restraints were inherently dangerous and had "too often led to tragedy." It banned all forms of neck restraints.

U.S. Attorney General Merrick Garland explained that the ban was more than just a matter of the department following prudent proven medical advice. It was also a matter of defusing the anger and mistrust the use of techniques such as the chokehold played in poisoning relations between law enforcement and minority communities,

"Building trust and confidence between law enforcement and the public we serve is central to our mission at the Justice Department." "The limitations implemented today on the use of 'chokeholds,' [and] 'carotid restraints' [...], are among the important steps the department is taking to improve law enforcement safety and accountability."

Biden and the Justice Departments' action on the chokehold was a case where political officials took heed of the advice from doctors, scientists, and medical experts about a lethal police technique that caused injury and death. They certainly got it right about a deadly tactic that maims and kills. The majority of those were Black and Hispanic men. That was a good step forward. But as many police reform advocates were quick to note only a step.

3
The Chokehold in Court

"Past exposure to illegal conduct,"

SCOTUS Justice Byron White in a majority opinion on a lawsuit on the chokehold stated, "does not permit someone to seek an injunction." He further added, "Lyons' standing to seek the injunction requested depended on whether he was likely to suffer future injury from the use of the chokeholds by police officers."

White was speaking for a majority of the justices in rejecting the lawsuit brought by Alfred Lyons in 1976 to bar the LAPD from using the chokehold. At the time, hundreds of men had been subjected to the hold by the LAPD. There were multiple deaths. Nearly all of the victims were Black.

Byron's court colleague, Thurgood Marshall, didn't agree with the majority, "the evidence submitted to the District Court established that, for many years, it has been the official policy of the city to permit police officers to employ chokeholds in a variety of situations where they face no threat of violence."

White's view held. And that effectively closed the door on any immediate prospect of scrapping the chokehold as a police tactic. Even so,

Marshall saw the mortal danger in the decision, "if the police adopt a policy of 'shoot to kill,' or a policy of shooting 1 out of 10 suspects, the federal courts will be powerless to enjoin its continuation."

Lyons was one of the victims of police misconduct. Fortunately, he did not die after being subjected to a chokehold. However, it set in motion the legal challenge that wound its way up to the SCOTUS. Lyons simply sought a court injunction against the hold. Lyons, like Eric Garner and George Floyd, was a young African American male. Lyons was not stopped for a felony offense, or a violent act. It was a routine traffic stop.

*****

The case appeared solid on several grounds. He could show a disparate use of the hold against African Americans. The LAPD had used the chokehold with impunity for years and the victims were mostly Blacks. It appeared to fall under the purview of the constitutional provision barring cruel and unusual punishment.

In sworn testimony, officers made jokes and wisecracks about how some suspects placed in the chokehold danced and squirmed uncontrollably. There was convincing evidence that many officers who used the hold did not know the lethal effect of the hold and their training officers did not bother to tell them of the life-threatening danger of the hold.

One officer described in graphic and painful detail the effect of a chokehold. He noted that the victim's face turns blue as he is deprived of oxygen. He goes into spasmodic convulsions. His eyes rolled back. His body wriggles. His feet kick up and down. His arms move about wildly.

Lyons survived but he was severely injured because of the hold. The case meandered through the courts for years and the LAPD publicly claimed that it had temporarily suspended the use of the hold pending a high court decision. Meanwhile, other police departments continued to use it with no legal or departmental restraints.

The death toll continued to mount. In 1983, the court finally spoke. In a majority opinion, it ruled that a federal court had no power to prohibit the use of the hold. It didn't stop there. Even more stunningly, it said that a real and immediate threat that he would again be stopped. . .by an officer who would illegally choke him into unconsciousness." Translated, a victim could be choked by a police officer, and the choke posed no threat to the victim. Further, he could be subject to its use if stopped again.

Marshal in his blistering dissent blasted this as absurd: "Since no one can show that he will be choked in the future, no one—not even a person who, like Lyons, has almost been choked to death—has standing to challenge the continuation of the policy."

This was a license to choke and to no surprise, Gates crowed victory. He claimed that it vindicated his contention that the chokehold was an appropriate tactic to be used. However, the Los Angeles Police Commission and L.A. city officials stepped in, read the handwriting on the wall, and barred the use of the hold.

*****

That didn't end the matter. Nearly a decade after the LAPD officially barred the use of the hold, the issue reared up again following the beating of Black motorist Rodney King in March 1991. The LAPD debated whether to reinstate the chokehold on the grounds it was a less lethal way to subdue a suspect. Though the ban stayed in effect, surveys found that most officers backed the use of the hold and said they saw no danger in its use.

For the next nearly half-century following the SCOTUS ruling permitting the use of chokeholds, the chokehold remained a crucial weapon in police arsenals. There were few legal challenges to its use. That changed with the chokehold death of Eric Garner in 2014 and the non-indictment of the officer who applied the hold. Some police departments and police oversight groups scrambled fast. They either barred or recommended the barring of the chokehold.

That was not the end of the chokehold story. Incredibly, many police departments continued to sanction use of the chokeholds and similar potentially lethal methods of restraint.

The NYPD was one of them. Police officials there sanctioned the hold. Predictably, the complaints from victims soared and the injuries from the use of the hold climbed. In 2020, under intense pressure to ban the hold, city officials acted.

They made it a criminal misdemeanor to use a restraint method that restricts the flow of air or blood by compressing the windpipe or carotid arteries or by sitting, kneeling, or standing on the chest or back "in a manner that compresses the diaphragm."

However, as usual, even that didn't end the matter. Police unions sued to have the hold reinstated. They lost the first round. In June 2021, the New York State Supreme Court upheld the ban. The unions appealed. The case went back to the state high court's appeals court. It reversed the high court's decision. It called the ban "unnecessarily vague."

Police unions contested the ban on the seemingly innocuous and technical grounds that it was difficult if not impossible for officers to judge whether their action in using the chokehold was causing physical harm. The Appellate Court agreed.

NYPD officials contended that their training tactics in the use of the hold were so strict that the chokehold would not cause injury or death. The Appellate Court agreed again.

"That (the NYPD policies) are stricter than the statute itself – prohibiting any sitting, kneeling, or standing on an individual's torso regardless of the effect – is not proof that the diaphragm compression language is incapable of being understood," the decision stated, "The police may simply be seeking to hold themselves to a higher standard or to err on the side of caution, as they did even before the enactment of this law."

However, the Appellate Court did not have the final word. The State Supreme Court stepped back in and upheld the ban.

Still, the Appellate Court's decision to reverse the ban on the chokehold sent a clear message and signal. The message was that the courts despite the push for police reforms, among which was the banning of the chokehold, were still prepared to give wide license to police departments to subvert reforms. Again, one of which was the use of the chokehold.

The ominous signal the SCOTUS and the New York state court's ruling sent was that police departments still had total discretion regarding when and what tactics they could use. That included the use of the chokehold.

*****

Ironically, many of the same issues that toiled the courts and police department regarding the chokehold arose when ex-Marine Daniel Penny was arrested and charged with second-degree manslaughter in the choking death on a Manhattan subway train on May 1, 2023.

In this case, there was much debate over whether the charge of manslaughter was much too light with a whiff of racial bias. Or was it indeed, the right charge given the circumstance? A prominent civil attorney examined the charge against Penny. He detailed what he believed the severity in which Penny applied the chokehold merited the harsher charge of second-degree murder. Here is his argument.

"The implication of such a charge was that the death of Neely was the result of some accidental event devoid of malice that somehow went wrong and was somehow unforeseeable. This, of course, ignores the fact that the chokehold, as taught to Penny, is inherently dangerous in both its deployment and implementation. In fact, the local medical examiner has determined that the cause of death of Neely was death by "compression of the neck" which is the design function of the choke hold.

1. Intent to Kill

2. Killing committed during an Inherent Dangerous Felony

3. Intent to Commit Serious Bodily Harm

4. Depraved Heart

The above mechanisms were based on what is called the Model Penal Code that is taught to law students across the land.

The actions of Daniel Penny would qualify as numbers 3 and 4.

Under the New York Penal Code Section 125.25, which can be accessed at the link, https://www.nysenate.gov/legislation/laws/PEN/125.25 there are three ways to show intent to kil

1. Intent to Cause the death of another person

2. Deprave Indifference to Human Life/Recklessness resulting in death

3. Robbery, Burglary, kidnapping, arson, or rape that results in a death

Specific to New York, Penny would qualify as a murderer under #2.

Why?

He used a chokehold. There are two kinds of chokeholds: blood choke and air choke. The blood choke restricts blood flow to the brain and can make a person go unconscious within 13 seconds. The air choke, on the other, can cut off the blood and the air to the brain. This is accomplished by crushing the trachea (the windpipe). In other words, it compresses the neck.

The cause of death for Jordan Neely was "compression of the neck".

Under New York Penal Code 125.25 a person is guilty of murder when "under circumstances evincing a depraved indifference to human life, he recklessly engages in conduct which creates a grave risk of death to another person, and thereby causes the death of another person".

The chokehold cuts off the blood (the flow of life) and air (the breath of life) to a human being when employed in the manner that Daniel Penny was taught to use (and not use) by the United States Marine Corps. Neely was unconscious after 8 minutes. Penny pressed on nevertheless completely evincing a "depraved indifference" to Neely's state of unconsciousness to the point that Neely died at the fifteen-minute mark.

Like all penal codes, there are defenses. However, Penny was not attacked by Neely nor did Neely lay hands, spit, lunge, slap, touch, kick, bite, or physically have contact with anyone on that train. The reports so far that Nelly was yelling and harassing passengers and had not threatened anyone in particular. No witness has come forward to report any injuries or the need for medical treatment. No weapon has been discovered.

While a Murder 2 conviction may be challenging given the prejudice that exists against homeless Black men, it is not impossible. Indeed, overcharging is the standard protocol in criminal prosecutions. In this case, this would not be an "overcharge" at all."

The Floyd slaying and before that, the Garner slaying did nothing to change the fact that the chokehold was still not a thing of the legal past. The murder of Neely by a chokehold even by a civilian and the widespread public applauding of its use not to mention the contention by many that the charge of manslaughter was an undercharge was even more unsettling evidence of that.

4
The Chokehold Under Attack

"**I** don't like chokeholds," Then President

Trump said in an interview that aired on *Fox News*, "Sometimes, if you're alone and you're fighting someone, it's tough,"
"It would be, I think, a very good thing that, generally speaking, it should be ended."

Trump's *Fox News* interview in June 2020, came one month after the choking slaying of Floyd. So, even Trump had good reason to voice his wariness of the chokehold. It had less to do with Floyd's death than the by-then mounting number of deaths and injuries to civilians from the use of chokeholds.

Even before Floyd's death, the names of the victims whose deaths resulted from chokeholds continued to lengthen. In some cases, they drew protests, national attention, hefty lawsuits, and continuing calls for banning the hold. The men whose chokehold-related deaths drew public attention were James Thompson in Chicago, Allen Simpson in Dallas, Rodney Lynch in Gallup, New Mexico, Dustin Boone in Las Vegas, Roger Owensby Jr. in Cincinnati, Carl Glen Wheat in Amarillo, Texas, Gerald Arthur in New Orleans and Torris Harris in Chattanooga, Tennessee.

In the aftermath of the Garner slaying in 2014, these cases were costing cities a lot of money and legal headaches to resolve the dubious deaths. In each case, there were lawsuits. The demands were not solely for monetary damages but to prevent departments from continuing to use the chokehold.

The cases were hard fought and often tough to win. They required proof that the officer that used a chokehold crossed the line between a legitimate tactic to prevent harm or injury to someone and gross negligence.

The victims' only recourse to skirt the high bar to win a suit was to argue that the chokehold violated the victim's constitutional guarantee of freedom of Fourth Amendment rights. This bars unlawful searches and seizures by law enforcement. In this case, the search and seizure against were not property but the victim's person.

A 1985 SCOTUS decision in *Tennessee v. Garner* (1985) opened the legal door for a chokehold use lawsuit on Fourth Amendment grounds. The court was clear. Police could only use the chokehold among other deadly force tactics only "to prevent the escape of a fleeing suspect" and "only if the officer has a good-faith belief that the suspect poses a significant threat of death or serious physical injury to the officer or others."

This latter stipulation was crucial. Police officials that defended the use of the chokehold repeatedly contended that their officers did not spuriously use the chokehold but only as practically a last resort to prevent severe injury to the officer or innocent civilians. This rationale reduced the question of how successful a lawsuit could be to a subjective judgment call by the officers. Thus, the courts had to decide whether, or how much of a safety threat a suspect put in a chokehold posed to the officer or others.

Despite the high bar, cases such as the Garner slaying and the chokehold slaying by the Las Vegas Police of Tashi Brown in 2017 resulted in substantial settlements. New York shelled out nearly six million dollars to the

Garner family and Las Vegas paid over two million dollars to Brown's family.

In 2015, police departments in the nation's ten largest cities were on the financial hook for a quarter billion dollars in payouts to the families of victims of chokeholds and related misconduct cases. This represented a nearly fifty percent jump in the number of and dollar amount of lawsuits and settlements in these cases.

*****

There was no end in sight in these cases despite the mounting department bans. A case in point. Two weeks before Penny choked Neely to death, the family of Joel Acevedo demanded more than six million dollars in compensation from the Milwaukee police department for the chokehold slaying of Acevedo. He died after a chokehold restraint was placed on him in April 2020.

The lawsuit made five specific allegations. Among them was that the chokehold was an "unconstitutional policy and custom." It showed "deliberate indifference." And that it was a horrible example of the use of deadly force without justification.

The added twist was that the lawsuit blamed the department for encouraging officers to use the chokehold. The further irony was that the Milwaukee Police and Fire Commission a year after Acevedo's death issued a public statement decrying the use of the chokehold. It undoubtedly had one eye on the furor over the Floyd chokehold slaying. And another on the potentially staggering costs of lawsuits and settlements in chokehold death cases.

It didn't take long after the Acevedo case filing to see why police and public officials were increasingly nervous and unsettled in finding themselves on the financial hook for costly payouts in chokehold use lawsuits. One week after the Penny choking slaying of Neely and a month after the Acevedo multimillion-dollar lawsuit, California paid out twenty-four million dollars in a lawsuit settlement to the family of Edward Bronstein.

Bronstein also was a chokehold victim. His case made national news for two reasons. He screamed, "I Can't Breathe." These were the same words that Floyd screamed when he was being choked to death. Bronstein died after restraints were applied by multiple California Highway Patrol officers following an altercation in March 2020.

The Los Angeles County coroner said Bronstein's death was caused by "acute methamphetamine intoxication during restraint by law enforcement." The other twist was that Bronstein was white.

Seven California Highway Patrol officers and a nurse were charged with involuntary manslaughter in March 2023 in his death. The dollar amount was the biggest payout by the state in a death related to police misconduct.

The case and settlement saw another pattern in chokehold cases. It prompted a policy change. CHP officials quickly announced that it would prevent its officers from using techniques or transport methods that involve a substantial risk of positional asphyxia."

The state followed suit. In September 2021, a year after Bronstein's death, California Governor Gavin Newsom signed a law barring police from using certain face-down holds that have led to multiple unintended deaths. That was a polite, legalese way of saying chokeholds and other types of neck restraints were deadly.

The costly mix of public and media odor of chokeholds, the Floyd slaying, and jitters over having to ladle out tens of millions in settlements and the costs of fighting lawsuits finally resulted in a reform long needed.

That was to slap a limitation or complete ban on a technique that by 2023 had become the flashpoint of national concern and anger.

5

Penny, the Marines, and the "Blood Choke"

It was taking your pick: scary, nerve-racking, and potentially lethal. All of that and more almost certainly flowed through the mind of Platoon 3075 guide Recruit Timothy Palmer when he popped open an eye after being subjected to a chokehold in a Marine training camp. Fortunately, Palmer suffered no injury after platoon mate Recruit Kale Minkie released his rear chokehold on him.

This was just a demonstration of the chokehold technique known as the rear choke and the figure-4 variation choke. These are the two chokeholds Marines are taught and they must master. During the training in the use of this chokehold, Marine trainers continually emphasize that the chokehold can do great bodily harm if it is not properly executed. In fact, the Marine manual warns, "These techniques are dangerous, but recruits must apply them in training to confirm mastery."

Still, each time a Marine trainee was subjected to the hold they invariably cringe when in the grip of the python-like blood choke. Marine

recruit Wayne Robinson pulled no punches in describing his feeling when he was wrapped in the hold,
"When he squeezed, I felt tingling around my brain. I was red in the face, and I got really lightheaded." The Marine training manual on the use of the two chokeholds details exactly what and how the Marines teach the two holds.

The choker wraps his bicep and forearm around the opponent's neck, clasps his hands together, and squeezes in the rear choke. The other chokehold taught the figure-4 variation which uses almost the same technique. The one difference is that the choker places their hand on the choking arm is which placed on the opposite bicep. The other hand goes behind the opponent's head.

The manual does not attempt to pose one of the choke techniques as benign and harmless. It categorizes both as "blood chokes." Both, according to the manual, can stop blood flow to the brain. This can kill.

The Marines teach the two lethal choke holds in order as the manual states to "incapacitate the enemy faster." Incapacitation normally takes eight to 13 seconds to work." The Marine manual also makes clear that the "blood choke" hold is solely geared toward "combat situations" where speed, brute force, and physical harm, are the watchwords in taking down "the enemy."

Marine instructors give meticulous demonstrations and instructions to Marine recruits before they are allowed to practice applying the techniques. They do it by the "numbers" which means that they count out each step that is used in the technique as a fail-safe method to ensure that the technique is used properly and safeguard against injury. The instructors watch closely to make sure that they apply the pressure slowly and carefully to their opponent's neck.

An added safeguard is if the Marine recruit that's subject to the hold feels physical endangerment, he or she can tap the choker. At that point, they must release the hold. "When we teach any chokes or holds, the tap-out rule always applies," said an instructor. The instructors constantly walk through the ranks of recruits that are being trained to make sure that they are following the safety rules.

*****

That's hardly the case, though, in actual combat situations. There the expectation is that the hold be applied quickly and with force. A Marine instructor explained, "We apply slow pressure in training because a jolting, crushing squeeze could collapse the trachea. But in combat, a jolting squeeze is ideal."

There is one more crucial component in the Marine training on the chokehold. The choker is not allowed to hold the choke for more than five seconds. Daniel Penny held his Marine-taught "blood choke" on Neely for at least eight minutes. That was something that the Marines did not teach Penny.

6

Revisiting the City of Los Angeles v. Lyons

When Alfred Lyons sued the city of

Los Angeles in 1976, he sought an injunction to bar the use of the chokehold. He had been subjected to and suffered severe injury. At first glance, the case appeared solid on several grounds. He could show a disparate use of the hold against African Americans.

The LAPD had used the chokehold with impunity for years, and in one span the majority of the sixteen of the victims that died as a result of the chokehold were black. This appeared to fall under the purview of the constitutional provision barring cruel and unusual punishment.

The case meandered through the courts for years. This is the detail of how the high court finally disposed of the case and why it still reverberated with disastrous consequences decades afterward.

Citation. *22 Ill.461 U.S. 95, 103 S. Ct. 1660, 75 L. Ed. 2d 675 (1983)*

Brief Fact Summary. *Adolph Lyons (Lyons) was pulled over by a Los Angeles police officer for a traffic violation. He offered no resistance, and* *without provocation, the police officer seized Lyons and placed him in a chokehold, rendering Lyons unconscious.*

Synopsis of Rule of Law. *A plaintiff who wants to invoke the jurisdiction of the Supreme Court must allege an "actual case or controversy." Further, the injury complained of by the plaintiff must be immediate. Past exposure to illegal conduct does not, by itself, show a present case or controversy.*

The speculative nature of Plaintiff's claim of future injury requires a finding that this prerequisite of equitable relief has not been fulfilled.

Facts. *In 1976, Lyons was pulled over by a Los Angeles police officer for a traffic violation. Although Lyons offered no resistance, the officer asked him to step out of the car and proceeded to place Lyons in a* *chokehold, rendering Lyons unconscious. Lyons sued the municipality and sought damages and injunctive relief in District Court for the Central District of California.*

He asked the court to issue an injunction preventing the police department from using chokeholds in the future unless circumstances were to result in death or serious bodily injury if force was withheld. The District Court entered such an injunction. The Court of Appeals for the Ninth Circuit affirmed. The municipality appealed to the Supreme Court.

Issue. *Does this case present an "actual case or controversy" that can be determined by the Supreme Court?*

If so, does Lyons have standing to seek injunctive relief against the municipality of Los Angeles?

Held. *This case does not present an "actual case or controversy" as required in the Constitution under Article III. Past illegal conduct, by itself, is insufficient to establish an actual case or controversy for injunctive relief. Even though Lyons was injured by the police in the past, this act alone does not establish that Lyons is threatened with immediate injury or that he will be pulled over and placed in a chokehold again.*

Lyons did not have standing to bring this case to the Supreme Court. To have standing, a plaintiff must show 1) an actual or likely injury in fact, 2) that the injury is sufficiently concrete and individually affects the plaintiff, 3) that the challenged action is the "cause in fact" of the injury, and 4) that the Court will be able to redress the injury by its decision. In this case, injunctive relief against the municipality may or may not address the injury suffered by Lyons.

He could seek damages for any injuries he sustained from the chokehold (i.e., hospital bills, etc.), but he did not have standing to enforce an injunction where it was not clear if others would be placed in a chokehold in the future. Furthermore, it was speculative, at best, that Lyons himself would be placed in a chokehold in the future, and therefore injunctive relief would not clearly redress any potential injury.

Dissent. *Lyons did have standing to bring a claim for injunctive relief against the municipality because he did present an actual case or controversy and had suffered damages relating to the chokehold. Standing has always depended on whether a plaintiff has a "personal stake in the outcome of the controversy." The Dissent explained that*

Lyons' request for injunctive relief was coupled with his claim for damages based on past injury. Because he has an actual claim for damages, he need not rely solely on the threat of future injury to establish his stake in the outcome of the controversy.

Discussion. *Past exposure to illegal conduct does not, by itself, establish a present case or controversy, and therefore cannot meet the Article III Constitutional requirement of "actual case or controversy."*

*****

In the immediate aftermath of Lyon's initial filing of the lawsuit, the LAPD publicly claimed that it had temporarily suspended the use of the hold pending the high court's decision hold. But other police departments continued to use the chokehold with no legal or departmental restraints. The death toll continued to mount.

Again, in the four decades since the high court refused to bar the use of the hold the record still is that there is nothing in law or public policy that officially precludes any police department from putting the chokehold or a variation of it back in its weapons arsenal. That remained the case before, during, and after Garner, then Floyd, then Neely became the poster men for the chokehold and its deadly consequence.

Conclusion
The Chokehold—Alive and Well

George Floyd was slain in May 2020 by a chokehold administered by then-Minneapolis police officer Derek Chauvin. In the four months after thirty-two of the nation's sixty-five largest police departments either clamped a total ban or severely restricted the use of neck restraints.

Before Floyd's murder, the Los Angeles Police Department banned the hold in 1983, and the Chicago Police Department and the Houston Police Department banned it in 2014 following the chokehold murder of Eric Garner. The Philadelphia Police Department banned it in 2020.

The nation's largest police department, the NYPD at least on paper in 1993 banned chokeholds. The ban followed the chokehold-related death of a suspect by traumatic asphyxia while in police custody in 1991.

President Biden issued an Executive Order in 2022 barring the use of the chokehold by federal law enforcement agencies. The exception was it could be used if there was a dire life-threatening situation to the officer. However, more than half of the nation's police departments in 2023 still either permitted the use of chokeholds or some form of neck restraint. The

SCOTUS and the New York State Supreme Courts Appellate Court Division tossed the NYPD chokehold ban following a lawsuit by that city's police unions in 2021. The chokehold ban was always at or near the top of the list of reforms that police reform advocates for years had clamored for.

*****

There were two prime reasons why the use of the chokehold survived despite the many deaths and injuries from its use. And despite the nearly unanimous opinion by doctors, and medical experts that chokeholds no matter how well trained the officer, or how benign the restraint, still posed a grave risk of causing severe injury or death.

The first was that police unions backed by a large segment of the public were vehement in their contention that the chokehold was a useful and necessary technique to fight crime and protect the officer and others from greater harm. The other unstated, but lurking beneath the surface, was race.

The majority of those killed or maimed by chokeholds were African American or Hispanic men. That fit in with the public narrative that violent crime still came largely with a Black or Hispanic male face. Therefore, any and every weapon the police could store in their crime-fighting arsenal was fair game for use in combatting the crime menace with the added and subtle racial twist to it.

The murder of Jordan Neely by ex-Marine Daniel Penny using a lethal chokehold did not change the narrative. Neely had a lengthy arrest record, was homeless, had mental challenges, and was a Black male. Though Penny was arrested and charged with the chokehold death, the groundswell of support for him underscored the fact that much of the public saw nothing wrong, indeed applauded, the use of the restraint that Penny applied to Neely, which ultimately killed him.

The grim truth remained. Garner, Floyd, and Neely all met their deaths through chokeholds. Each death ignited outrage and calls for a total ban on it. Yet, the chokehold remained very much alive and well. Worse, there was no hopeful sign that that would likely change.

Sources

Ian Millhiser, "How the Supreme Court enable Police to use Deadly Chokeholds," *Vox*, May 30, 2020

https://www.vox.com/2020/5/30/21274697/supreme-court-police-chokehold-george-floyd-derek-chauvin-lyons-los-angeles

William Raspberry, "The Chief and the Chokehold," *Washington Post*, May 17, 1982

https://www.washingtonpost.com/archive/politics/1982/05/17/the-chief-and-the-choke-hold/e17fa90f-c692-43c2-935f-463da9cab500/

Emma Tucker, "Bans on chokeholds for federal officers latest in nationwide push to hold police to a 'higher standard'," *CNN*, September 15, 2021 https://www.cnn.com/2021/09/15/us/police-accountability-george-floyd/index.html

"Use of Carotid Technique," *Public Safety Canada,* March 22, 2021

https://www.publicsafety.gc.ca/cnt/trnsprnc/brfng-mtrls/prlmntry-bndrs/20210722/032/index-en.aspx

Brandon Tensley, "The Supreme Court has sided with the police at the expense of Black Americans," *CNN,* August 26, 2021 https://www.cnn.com/2021/08/26/politics/policing-supreme-court-race-deconstructed-newsletter/index.html

James Santiago Grisolia, "What Chokeholds Can Do to the Brain," *Medical Page Today*, June 11, 2020
https://www.medpagetoday.com/publichealthpolicy/generalprofessionalissues/87008

Von Kleim, "Top Medical Experts Explore Safety of Vascular Neck Restraint. Will Their Finds Matter?" *Force Science*, November 2022

https://www.forcescience.com/2022/11/top-medical-experts-explore-safety-of-vascular-neck-restraints/

Asmae Fahmy, "Neurologists Call for an End to Police Neck Restraints, " *verywellhealth.com,* January 13, 2021 https://www.verywellhealth.com/neurologists-viewpoint-police-use-of-neck-restraints-5094737

C.J. Ciaramella, "Biden Signs Executive order restricting Chokeholds," *Reason,* May 25, 2022

https://reason.com/2022/05/25/biden-signs-executive-order-restricting-chokeholds-and-limiting-transfer-of-military-equipment-to-police/

Ian Millhiser, "How the Supreme Court enable Police to use Deadly Chokeholds," *Vox*, May 30, 2020

https://www.vox.com/2020/5/30/21274697/supreme-court-police-chokehold-george-floyd-derek-chauvin-lyons-los-angeles

Mark Morales, "New York State Supreme Court Ruling Reinstates Law Banning Police Officers from Using chokeholds during arrests, "*CNN*, May 19, 2022

https://www.cnn.com/2022/05/19/us/nypd-chokehold-diaphragm-ban-state-supreme-court-ruling/index.html

"Trump Says He Generally Opposes Police Chokeholds, Stops Short of Supporting Ban," *NPR*, June 12, 2020

https://www.npr.org/sections/live-updates-protests-for-racial-justice/2020/06/12/876173108/trump-says-he-generally-opposes-police-chokeholds-stops-short-of-supporting-ban

"Lawsuits for Police Chokehold Deaths," *The National Law Review*, November 23, 2020 https://www.natlawreview.com/article/lawsuits-police-chokehold-deaths

Drew Dawson, "Family of Joel Acevedo Sues 2 Former Milwaukee Officers,

ex-Chief for Wrongful Death," *Milwaukee Journal Sentinel*, April 14, 2023

https://www.jsonline.com/story/news/2023/04/14/family-sues-2-former-milwaukee-officers-ex-chief-in-fatal-chokehold/70114809007/

"California to Pay $24 Million Settlement to family of man who died after violent arrest," *CBS*, May 9, 2023

https://www.cbsnews.com/news/edward-bronstein-california-settlement-violent-arrest-death-involuntary-manslaughter-chp-officers/

"USMC Choking Techniques," *theusmarines.com*, nd

https://theusmarines.com/journals/usmc-choking-techniques/

"City of Los Angeles v. Lyons, "*CaseBriefs*, nd

https://www.casebriefs.com/blog/law/constitutional-law/constitutional-law-keyed-to-cohen/the-jurisdiction-of-federal-courts-in-constitutional-cases/city-of-los-angeles-v-lyons/

Brandon Tensley, "The Supreme Court has sided with the police at the expense of Black Americans," *CNN*, August 26, 2021

The Supreme Court has repeatedly sided with the police. Black Americans are paying the price | CNN Politics

Ty Roush, "Why Chokeholds Used by Daniel Penny on Jordan Neely are Increasingly Banned by Police Departments," *Forbes,* May 12, 2023

https://www.forbes.com/sites/tylerroush/2023/05/12/why-chokeholds-used-by-daniel-penny-on-jordan-neely-are-increasingly-banned-by-police-departments/?sh=761abc974aa2

Bibliography

Balko, Radley, *Rise of the Cop Warrior-The Militarization of America's Police Forces*, (New York, 2021)

Butler, Paul, *Chokehold: Policing Black Men*, (New York, 2017)

Chemerinsky, Erwin, *Presumed Guilty: How the Supreme Court Empowered the Police and Subverted Civil Rights*, (New York, 2021)

Gaines, Larry K., et.al, *Policing in America* (New York, 2021)

Hinton, Elizabeth, *America on Fire-The Untold History of Police Violence and Black Rebellion Since the 1960s*, (New York, 2021)

Jackson, Thomas, *Policing Ferguson, Policing America* (Skyhorse, 2017)

Klarman, Michael J, *From Jim Crow to Civil Rights: The Supreme Court and the Struggle for Racial Equality*, (New York, 2006)

Reynold, Liam, *Justice for George Floyd-The Trial of Derek Chauvin and the Battle for Equality* (Amazon Kindle, 2023)

Index

About the Author

Earl Ofari Hutchinson is the author of multiple books on race and politics in America. He is a political analyst. He has appeared on MSNBC and on CNN. His books include the trilogy on the Obama Years: *The Obama Legacy, How Obama Governed; The Year of Crisis and Challenge*, and *How Obama Won.* His most recent books are The *Trump Challenge to Black America, From King to Obama: Witness to a Turbulent History* and *Bring Back the Poll Tax—The GOP War on Voting Rights*